Editors
Stephanie Buehler, M.P.W., M.A.
Gisela Lee

Editorial Manager
Karen J. Goldfluss, M.S. Ed.

Editor-in-Chief
Sharon Coan, M.S. Ed.

Illustrator
Chandler Sinnott

Cover Artist
Denise Bauer

Art Coordinator
Denice Adorno

Creative Director
Elayne Roberts

Imaging
Ralph Olmedo, Jr.
James Edward Grace

Product Manager
Phil Garcia

Publisher
Mary D. Smith, M.S. Ed.

Elections

Grades 1–3

Authors

*Stephanie Buehler, M.P.W., M.A. and
Kelley DosSantos Kremer*

Teacher Created Resources, Inc.
6421 Industry Way
Westminster, CA 92683
www.teachercreated.com.
ISBN: 978-1-57690-618-7
©2000 Teacher Created Resources, Inc.
Reprinted, 2008
Made in U.S.A.

Table of Contents

Introduction

Elections is a unit containing ideas and materials that will help teachers of primary grades instruct students about the concepts underlying our system of selecting leaders and changing laws. *Elections* connects students to the areas of language arts, social studies, math, and art through individual and cooperative group activities. The culminating activity, an election simulation, will help students further understand the concepts behind elections by asking them to utilize what they have learned in the preceding exercises as they take part in a classroom election. An important goal in this unit is to help the teacher impart in students a sense that they have an important responsibility to carry out when they become adults. As stated by a well-known election victor, Abraham Lincoln:

> *A child is a person who is going to carry on what you have started. He is going to sit where you are sitting and when you are gone, attend to those things which he thinks are important. You may adopt the policies you please, but how they are carried out depends on him. He will assume control of your cities, states, and nations. He is going to move in and take over your churches, schools, universities, and corporations . . . the fate of humanity is in his hands.*

Throughout this unit, you will find student pages with information and follow-up activities that will teach the basics of elections. The unit includes the following activities:

- conducting a secret election
- learning to vote wisely
- discussing and writing about the qualities of leadership
- creating campaign advertising
- understanding campaign fundraising
- creating graphs and a mapping activity related to elections
- conducting a poll or survey

In addition to these activities, creative outlets to expand students' imaginations are included. Students will also experience the election process through daily journal writing, artwork, and music.

At the end of the unit, a simulation activity will help students experience the election process in their own classroom from beginning to end.

A bibliography of helpful resources and Web sites is provided at the end of this unit.

Have You Voted?

Voting is a way people in a group make a decision. Have you ever voted in order to make a decision when several choices were available? Maybe your family voted on what type of ice cream to have for dessert, or maybe your friends voted whether to play jump rope or kickball at recess. Write or draw a picture of what you have voted for at home and at school.

Home

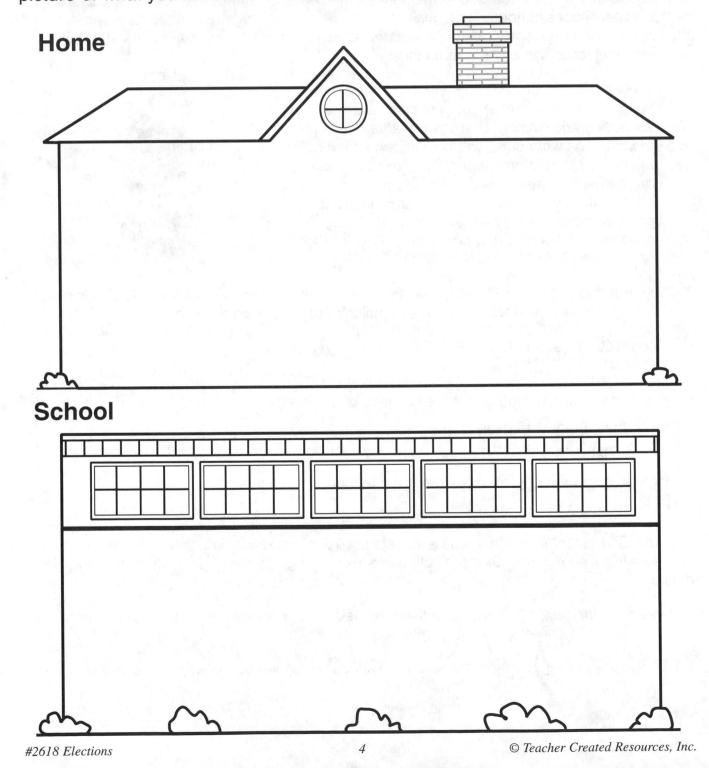

School

What Is an Election?

An **election** is an event when people make a choice between two or more people or things. In a political election, people vote, or make their choice known, for a person to hold a position in government. Positions, or offices of government include the President of the United States. Other offices are state leaders known as governors and city leaders known as mayors. There are also elections for offices of lawmakers, known as senators and representatives.

The act of voting is simple. In a political election, a voter marks a paper, called a ballot, next to the person to be chosen. The ballot goes into a ballot box. When the time to vote is over, the ballots are collected and counted. The person who gets the highest number or majority of votes is the winner.

There are other types of elections besides those for political office. People can vote for or against laws. People can vote to spend money for building things, such as schools. You yourself may have even voted for a favorite pet in a pet show or in some other type of election.

Elections can be held in a way that everyone can see how everyone else voted, or they can be held in secret. In a secret election, like those held in the United States, only the voter knows his or her own vote. You will participate in two activities to understand the difference.

Vote for your favorite pet!

Two Types of Elections

Ask students to read the information on page 5 before holding the two elections described below. (**Note:** Save the results of the elections for the graphing activity on page 8.)

Open Election

Most students have probably had the experience of voting, but this opener can remind them of the urgency to express their opinions and the ways in which those opinions influence their peers. Tell students that they will have a few votes and that they are permitted to look around them to see how their classmates are voting. As they vote, you might want to count aloud and/or make a tally on the chalkboard to drive home the point that everyone can see how everyone else voted. (Save the results.) Here are some suggestions for an informal vote:

Favorite color: red, blue, green, yellow, purple

Favorite flavor: apple, banana, cherry, grape, orange, pineapple

Favorite activity: playing sports, reading, seeing a movie, being with a pet, playing computer games

When you are finished, briefly discuss the experience. Which items were winners? Which choices did not receive winning votes? Do the children who voted for a winner feel great? Do the children who voted for a loser feel left out? Did anyone change their vote because he or she saw that a friend or someone else voted a certain way?

Secret Election

Some primary students lack impulse control—they are notorious peekers! Here is a peek-proof way to hold a truly secret election. You may find this activity easier to accomplish if you have an assistant or adult volunteer to help, but it is not necessary. First, copy the ballots on page 7 onto plain paper and cut the ballots. Have enough copies so that each student has one ballot. Ask students to line up outside the classroom door, then send students into the classroom one at a time. An assistant can help them mark the ballot, fold it, and put it into a box or basket, or you can place necessary items near the door so that you can easily direct each student to perform the secret task. Students who finish can be directed to their seats or back outside to the end of the line, where they can wait quietly. Remind them not to discuss their votes!

When everyone has voted, ask students to return to their seats if they have not done so already. Then count the votes in silence to make the point that this is a secret election. When you have counted all the votes, post the results on the chalkboard. (Remember to save the results.)

Discuss the results. Were there any surprises? Does it feel as good to win or as bad to lose when the election is secret? Was it harder to make a decision during a secret election? What are some good things about each kind of vote?

Secret Election Ballot

Secret Ballot

Mark your favorite.

Suckers

Jellybeans

Hard Sour Candy

Fruit Rolls

Secret Ballot

Mark your favorite.

Suckers

Jellybeans

Hard Sour Candy

Fruit Rolls

Election Graphing Activities

Use the results from the regular and secret votes that you and your classmates made to complete the following bar graphs. Write in the names of the things that you voted for and color the bars to show how many people voted for each thing. Give your graphs titles.

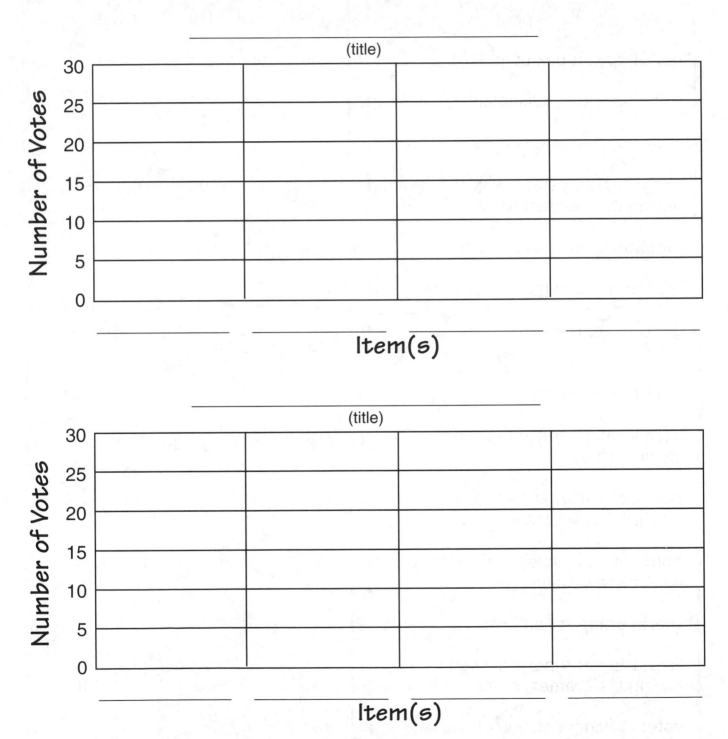

Note to Teacher: Make as many copies as you wish, asking students to create a graph for as many elections as you would like them to practice.

Basic Election Vocabulary

Directions: Study and use the following words with pages 10 and 11.

ballot: a sheet of paper which represents a list of candidates or issues

ballot box: a box used to hold ballots to be counted

candidate: a qualified citizen who runs for a political office

cast: to vote for a candidate or issue

Democrat: a person who is a member of one of the two political parties having the greatest number of members

election: process of selecting one or more persons by voting

graph: a visual representation of voting results

government: a name given to the lawmakers of the nation, state, or local area

majority: more than half of the total votes that are cast

nominee: person who is chosen to be a political party's candidate for an elected office

political party: an organization of people who share similar ideas and puts forward candidates for public offices

poll: counting votes in an election, a place where citizens vote, or a survey of citizen's opinions

representative: an individual who makes decisions on behalf of others

Republican: a person who is a member of one of the two political parties having the greatest number of members

vote: making a choice or decision in an election

Using Election Vocabulary

The more you are exposed to new vocabulary, the more likely you will use the new words in your own speech and writing. Use the definitions from page 9 or the words listed at the bottom of this page to help you complete the following sentences.

1. Mrs. Jones is voting by marking her choice on a paper called a
   _____.

2. People who share similar ideas about how to vote generally belong to the same _____.

3. The _____ of people voted for Nancy Smith, who was declared the winner late Tuesday night.

4. Casper Baker is sure to be chosen as his political party's
   _____.

5. A _____ taken last week showed that most people would vote to build a new courthouse in our county.

6. It is important to _____ so that you make your opinion known.

7. The best _____ on this year's ballot is Diane Newton.

8. Don't forget to _____ your ballot on Tuesday.

9. When you are finished voting, put your ballot in the
   _____.

Write three of your own sentences using election vocabulary.

1. _____

2. _____

3. _____

Election Vocabulary: ballot, ballot box, candidate, cast, Democrat, election, graph, government, majority, nominee, political party, poll, representative, Republican, vote

Election Vocabulary Word Search

Find the following election vocabulary words and phrases in the word search below.

ballot	election	political party
ballot box	graph	poll
candidate	government	representative
cast	majority	Republican
Democrat	nominee	vote

```
P O L I T I C A L P A R T Y
E D F M A J O R I T Y E P A
R B O R G Z C G T N V Q M O
E A L A R I X E V F O R S L
P L U C A N D I D A T E I C
U L Z A P B K Q E L E T R E
B O B S H A S T M H D W P L
L T N T P L C N O A V O B E
I B F U K L J F C X I M H C
C O W D G O V E R N M E N T
A X D M B T G Z A Q Q P Y I
N T A G Y S K J T O G O E O
Y J P N O M I N E E W L I N
V H M C H I U B N I K L R X
R E P R E S E N T A T I V E
```

Extensions: On a separate sheet, write a few sentences or a paragraph telling what you have learned about elections so far. See how many vocabulary words you can use in your writing.

Bonus: Find out what the symbols are for the two major U.S. political parties, Democrat and Republican. Draw and label them on a separate sheet.

Understanding Government

A **government** is a way of organizing people to do important jobs like making laws and protecting our country. When our United States government was first formed, its creators decided that a democracy would be the best type of government. A **democracy** is based on the idea that everyone is equal because everyone (of voting age) has a vote. Everyone can use his or her vote to make his or her choice known.

Sometimes it makes sense to elect one person who can then vote on many things. A **senator** is someone who is chosen to go to Washington, D.C., to hear about and vote on laws. The senator tries to vote in a way that the people who elected him or her expects. For example, people may elect a senator because he or she promises to vote on laws to help keep the air clean. The senator would then vote "yes" on the laws that would help clean up dirty air.

Not all countries have a democracy. For example, a country that has a king or queen as a ruler is called a **monarchy**. In some monarchies, the ruler makes all the decisions about laws and other matters. Over the ages, many people have fought wars in order to make their government a democracy. People all around the world want to vote to make their voices heard.

But democracies can have problems. Sometimes the people who vote and lose feel upset about how an election turns out. Sometimes a law to be voted on is hard to understand. Still, a democracy is a good form of government because it is fair to all people of a nation.

Extension: Use books to find information on one of the following topics. Define the word and then tell two or three facts related to it.

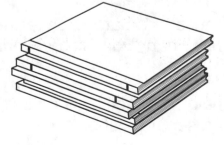

- **democracy**
- **monarchy**
- **senators**

- **representatives**
- **governor**
- **mayor**

12

What Are Polls?

Polls are an important part of the election process. Even young students may be exposed to polls when they watch television, listen to the radio, or see pie charts or other graphs in magazines or newspapers. Perhaps they have even seen their parent polled at a market or other place.

Explain to students that many candidates, or people running for government offices, use polls to help them understand how voters think or feel about something. In a way, a poll or a survey is like a pre-vote activity. People called "pollsters" will ask a voter his or her opinion on something, such as whether or not a new road should be built. With this information, candidates know how to talk to voters about an issue so that they will win votes.

You can help students understand the concept of a poll or survey by taking an impromptu one in the classroom. Write the following choices on poster board, overhead projector, or chalkboard, and then ask students the following question:

If we had 20 extra minutes of school every day, how should it be spent?

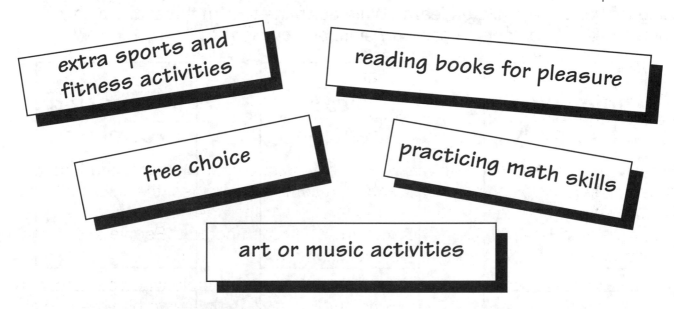

extra sports and fitness activities

reading books for pleasure

free choice

practicing math skills

art or music activities

To make this activity more like a simulation, you might break students into small groups, assigning one "pollster" to each group. Have the pollster ask each student in turn what his or her choice is. Collect and count the resulting polls.

So that students understand the difference between a vote and a poll, follow up with a discussion. When would be a good time to conduct a poll? (Before the election.) When is a vote held? (During an election.) Which results are "official," those from polls or those from votes? Also, try to direct students to see how someone running for office might use information from a poll to help them get votes. What things might a candidate say to get votes?

Continue the discussion on this important part of the election process by assigning the activity on page 14. Discuss the results of the poll. Ask what family members, in general, thought was most and least important to help children learn. Direct students to understand that a candidate for a school office might use this information to help him or her win the election by making a campaign promise or pledge.

Taking a Poll

When a poll is taken, it means that people are being asked about their opinions on a topic. This information can be used to help a candidate know what is important for voters. For example, a poll might ask people in a community if they would rather have a new airport or a new college built near their homes. If more people said that they wanted a new airport, then the candidate can tell people that he or she will vote to build one.

Take home this sheet to help you conduct a poll of family members. Be sure to return the sheet so that you can add your family members' opinions to the class poll. When everyone has returned their family polls, you can graph and discuss the overall results.

Ask each family member his or her opinion about what is the most important thing that can help children learn. Write down the total in the space below for each choice. Each person can only state one opinion.

quiet place to study	clear directions	interesting books
paying attention	practicing skills	tutoring

Extension: If you are able to do so, look in the newspaper or news magazines to find a poll. See if there is a chart or graph showing the information. Bring in a copy of the poll and/or graph to share with the class.

What Helps Children Learn?

(Graphing Information)

Use page 14 to conduct a poll of family members and return the sheet to school so that everyone's choices can be recorded and added together. Then use the information to complete the bar graph below. Color the corresponding number of boxes for each factor.

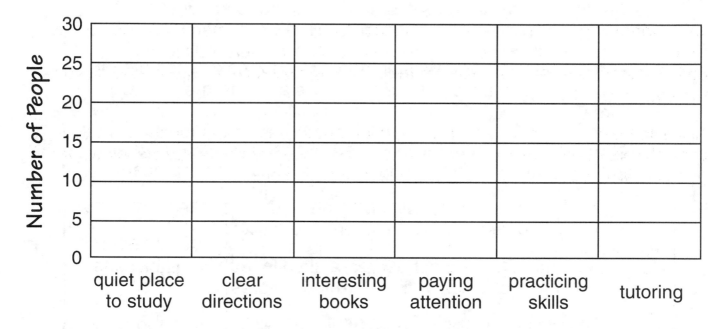

Factors That Help Children Learn

Answer the following questions:

1. Which category did people think was the most important for learning?

   _____

2. Which category did people think was the least important for learning?

   _____

3. Do you agree with most people about what is the most important item needed for learning? Why or why not? _____

   _____

   _____

Election Facts

What the Constitution Says

The Constitution is the document that lists the laws that govern the United States. Here are some basic facts to know about national elections.

✓ Representatives go to Washington, D.C., to make and vote on laws. Representatives are chosen by state voters every two years.

✓ Representatives must be at least 25 years old, United States citizens for seven years, and live in the state they represent.

✓ Senators, who also go to Washington, D.C., to make and vote on laws, are chosen by state voters every six years.

✓ Senators must be at least 30 years old, United States citizens for nine years, and live in the state they represent.

✓ The president must be at least 35 years old, a natural-born citizen, and have lived within the United States for 14 years.

✓ The president chooses the vice president.

✓ The person who will become president is chosen every four years.

✓ The president can only serve two terms, or eight years.

✓ Citizens of the United States are permitted to vote no matter what their race, color, or gender (male or female).

✓ Citizens of the United States are permitted to vote at age 18.

U.S. Representatives

While electing a president is perhaps the most important vote a citizen can make, there are other important national officials who must be elected. Each state holds an election to send two senators to the Senate in Washington, D.C., our nation's capital. Since there are 50 states, there are 100 senators.

Each state also sends a number of representatives to the House of Representatives, which is also in Washington, D.C. The number of representatives a state sends to Washington is based on its population, or the number of people living within it. The number of representatives each state sends can change as the population shrinks or grows. Some states have large populations, while others have populations that are quite small. Here is a chart showing an example of the number of representatives that are elected in 10 states. Use the chart below and the directions that follow to help you complete the map on page 18.

State	Number of Representatives
Alabama	7
California	53
Florida	25
Idaho	2
Massachusetts	10
New Jersey	13
New York	29
Pennsylvania	19
South Dakota	1
Wisconsin	8

Directions for U.S. Representatives Map:

1. Use a red crayon to color the state that has the most representatives as shown on the chart.

2. Use a purple crayon to color the state that has the fewest representatives as shown on the chart.

3. Use a yellow crayon to color the remaining states that have 25 or more representatives.

4. Use a green crayon to color the remaining states that have less than 25 representatives.

5. Use an orange crayon to color the District of Columbia, where Washington, D.C. is located.

Extension: Find out the name of the representative for the district in which you live. Write a class letter to this person and ask for information about what he or she is currently doing in our nation's capital.

U.S. Representatives Map

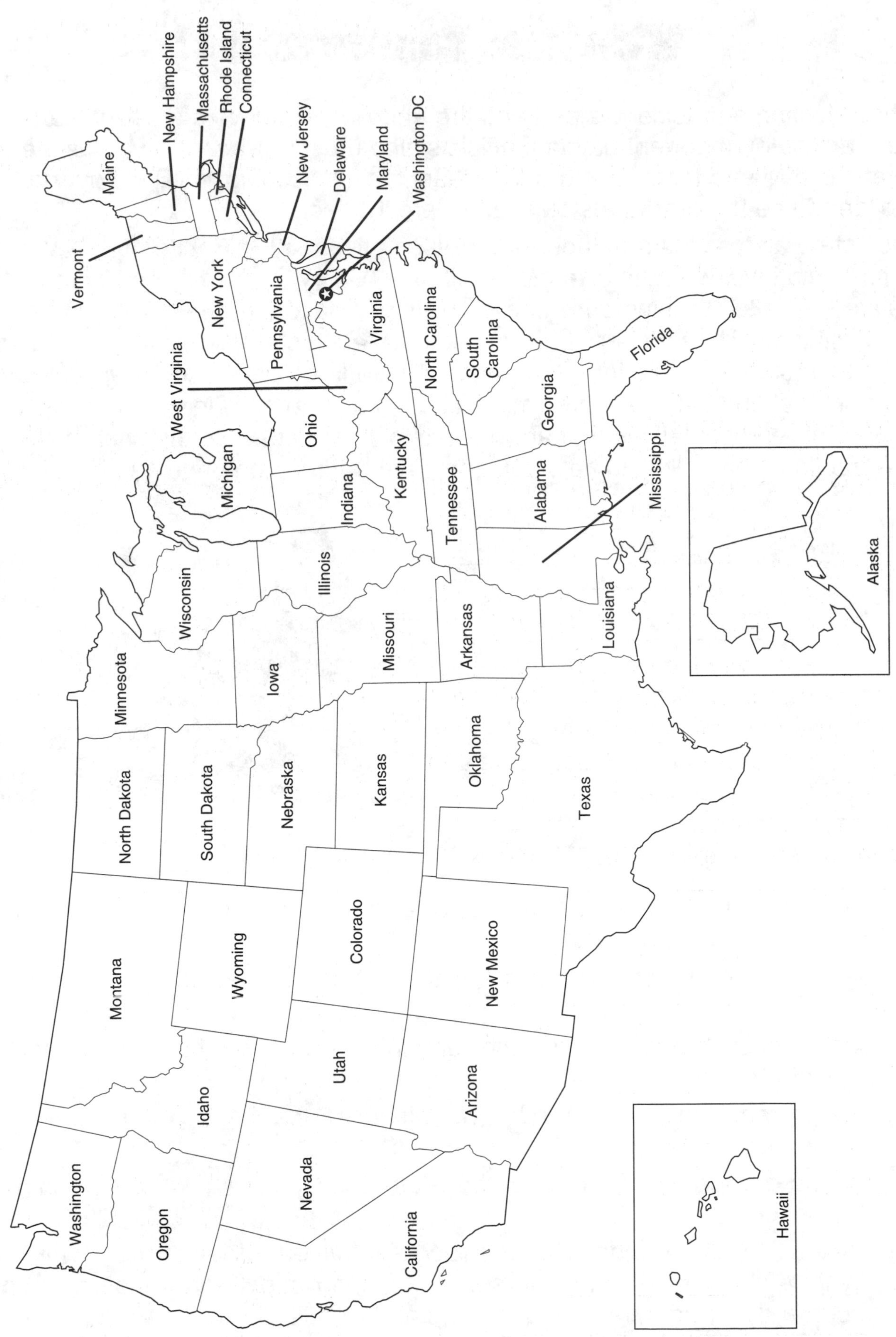

Vermont

Maine

New Hampshire
Massachusetts
Rhode Island
Connecticut

New Jersey
Delaware
Maryland
Washington DC

New York

Pennsylvania

Virginia

North Carolina

South Carolina

Florida

West Virginia

Ohio

Kentucky

Tennessee

Georgia

Alabama

Mississippi

Michigan

Indiana

Illinois

Wisconsin

Missouri

Arkansas

Louisiana

Minnesota

Iowa

Oklahoma

Texas

North Dakota

South Dakota

Nebraska

Kansas

Colorado

New Mexico

Montana

Wyoming

Washington

Oregon

Idaho

Nevada

Utah

Arizona

California

Alaska

Hawaii

18

What Do Leaders Do?

When voters elect a candidate, they are choosing someone to be a leader. The president, senators, representatives—all elected government officials—must have the ability to lead. But what do leaders do? Look at the following list of qualities to understand a leader's role.

- **Manage:** Leaders must know how to tell people to do certain jobs in order for work to get done.
- **Communicate:** Leaders must know how to speak and write in a way that promotes cooperation.
- **Convince:** Leaders must be able to lead people to hold beliefs that are similar to their own in order to get them to cooperate.
- **Make decisions:** Leaders must be able to understand a good deal of information in order to make sound decisions.
- **Enforce laws or rules:** Leaders generally have the power to make people— and even other leaders—obey laws.

Of course, not all leaders decide to run for office. There are many leaders all around you. Teachers, coaches, school principals, youth group leaders, and parents are examples of leaders with whom you are familiar.

Here is an activity that will help you think about what makes a person a leader. Select a leader that you know. Think about the roles of leaders, then think about how the person you know performs those roles. For example, if you pick a teacher, think about how the teacher communicates with students to get their cooperation. If you pick a coach, think about how that person convinces people on the team to believe that they will win. When you are finished writing, draw a picture of your leader. Share your work with your classmates.

_____
(name)

_____

_____

_____

_____

_____

_____

Promoting Leadership Qualities

Here is a list of suggestions to promote leadership qualities in your students.

- Find photographs of leaders in magazines or newspapers and create a bulletin board using them. Add to the bulletin board by listing important qualities that the leaders possess beneath each photograph.

- Discuss the question, "Are people born leaders, or can individuals be taught to be leaders?"

- Praise students who display leadership in daily activities.

- Discuss the moral obligations of leadership.

- Allow students to gain practice as leaders by providing opportunities through role-playing, cooperative group activities, and classroom responsibilities.

- Ask students if quiet people or verbal people make better leaders? Why do they think so? Are their beliefs correct or are they old ideas or stereotypes?

- Discuss different styles of leadership. These include, but are not limited to, leading by example and leading vocally.

- Organize mentor opportunities for your students with community leaders.

- Invite community leaders to speak to your class on what makes a good leader.

- Encourage students to read biographies.

- Ask students to complete the sheet entitled "Presidential Leaders" on page 21.

- Encourage students to interview leaders in their community, school, local government, or family.

- Discuss the importance of leaders in our society.

- Teach and allow your students to practice various skills associated with leadership. These include persuasive speaking and effective listening.

20

Presidential Leaders

The president of the United States has become the best known leader in the world. What do you know about any of the presidents who have been elected to office? Write a short report about a president by answering the questions. Draw a picture of the president you selected in the space provided.

Name of president:_____

President number:_____

Years in Office (Date)_____

Date of birth: _____

Place of birth: _____

Write three to five sentences with interesting information about this president that you did not know before.

_____

_____

_____

_____

_____

_____

_____

_____

_____

_____

Our Elected Officials

Fill in the blanks below with the names of your elected officials. You may need to use reference materials such as books, CD-ROMS, encyclopedias, the Internet, magazines, newspaper, etc.

Our Country:_____

President:_____

Vice President:_____

Senator: _____

Senator: _____

Representative: _____

Our State:_____

Governor: _____

Lt. Governor: _____

Legislator: _____

Legislator: _____

Our Community:_____

Mayor:_____

Councilperson: _____

Councilperson: _____

Other Elected Officials:_____

Campaign Advertising

A candidate who runs for office must have a way to get the word out as to why he or she will make a good leader. Voters also need to know why they should vote for or against certain laws.

Campaign information can be communicated in many ways. One way is through advertising on television, radio, or in the newspaper. Such advertising is paid for by the candidate's campaign fund.

Other more novel or fun ways to advertise are by using buttons, posters, or bumper stickers. Candidates also hold big pep rallies, which are parties where the candidate speaks and tries to get voters excited about voting for him or her.

Design a Poster

What makes a good campaign poster? A good poster is simple and uses few words. It needs to grab people's attention. A good poster uses bold colors and strong lines. Posters may have only a picture of the candidate and his or her name. Or a poster may have a single slogan, such as "Vote Ed, Not Fred." Design an eye-catching poster on a separate sheet of paper. The poster should feature the newest candidate in town—you! Try playing with your first or last name with rhyming words or words that sound similar in some way. See if you can come up with a catchy way (a slogan) for people to think about you.

Design a Bumper Sticker or Button

A good button or bumper sticker is even simpler than a poster. Election buttons and bumper stickers are often red, white, and blue. These colors alert people that the button or sticker is election related. Design a snappy button or bumper sticker for yourself using red, white, and blue as your color scheme. Your teacher can help you use a compass or a template to make a circle for a button.

Be a Wise Voter

Use this demonstration to help students realize the importance of knowing information before they vote. Copy enough ballots on this page so that each student can vote twice. Notice that the ballots differ in the amount of information they contain. Ballot A is the first ballot to be given to students. It contains only the names of possible candidates and proposed laws, also known as **propositions**. Ballot B, to be handed out either immediately or as soon as possible, is the second ballot that students will cast. It describes these candidates and laws in detail.

Pass out Ballot A and instruct students to mark their ballots. Most students will go ahead and vote without questioning the fact that they do not know for whom or for what they are voting. If someone does ask, simply state, "Please mark your ballot, and we will discuss your question later."

Collect Ballot A but do not yet show students any tally of their votes. Pass out Ballot B and ask students to vote again. You may read the descriptions aloud if some of your students are not yet reading but ask students not to speak to one another about their choices.

Collect Ballot B. Now tally the results of both ballots. Discuss any differences between the tallies. Why did they occur? Why is it important to be an informed voter? Why is it unwise to vote without having enough information?

Ballot A

Vote for one candidate.

Jim Fox ☐

Cecilia Ignacia Delgado ☐

Lisa Smith ☐

Wei Chang ☐

Vote *yes* or *no* for each proposition (law).

Proposition A

Yes ☐

No ☐

Proposition M

Yes ☐

No ☐

Ballot B

Vote for one candidate.

Jim Fox ☐
- Mr. Fox wants to sell park land to factories to create jobs.

Cecilia Ignacia Delgado ☐
- Mrs. Delgado wants to support people who build clean-air factories.

Lisa Smith ☐
- Mrs. Smith wants children to go to school year-round from 9 to 5.

Wei Chang ☐
- Mr. Chang wants to build more public parks where families can relax.

Vote once for each proposition.

Proposition A: This law would make it legal to ban reading from public places.

Yes ☐
No ☐

Proposition M: This law would prevent people who build offices from making ramps for wheelchairs.

Yes ☐
No ☐

Election Fundraising

Candidates need money to pay for the effort to run for office. Money is used to pay for staff people, such as secretaries and managers. Money is also needed to print and mail election information and for advertising. It is also used to pay for transportation when a candidate and his or her staff travel.

Money is raised in many ways. Sometimes people pay money to attend an event where a candidate will make a speech. Sometimes people send money to the campaign office or to the candidate's party. There are also "matching funds." This means that for each dollar that a candidate raises, they are given another dollar for spending to help them get elected.

There are limits to how much money a person or business can give to a candidate or to a cause. This prevents someone with a great deal of money from making the election unfair. For example, if one candidate was given a huge amount of money, he or she could buy lots and lots of advertising. The other candidate with less money could only buy less advertising. Soon everyone would know a lot about the wealthy candidate but not enough about the candidate with less money.

Do the following math problems alone or as a whole class while you think about campaign fundraising and the ways that candidates use money to get elected.

1. Candidate Jack Fremont must drive to the state capitol. A tank of gasoline costs $15. If he needs two tanks of gasoline, how much will gasoline cost for the trip? _____

2. Candidate Wilma Gray needs to buy paper for flyers announcing a pep rally. She needs to buy two packages of paper. Each package costs $2.45. How much money will she use for paper? _____

3. Poster board costs 15¢ per piece. Candidate Thomas Thatcher needs to make 10 posters. How much will it cost to make them? _____

4. a. Campaign buttons cost 5¢ apiece to make. How much does it cost to make five buttons? _____

   b. The buttons are sold at 10¢ apiece. How much money does it cost to buy five buttons? _____

   c. Now subtract the cost of making five buttons from the cost of buying five buttons. What is your answer? _____

Note: The answer you got in 4c is the candidate's profit from selling five buttons. The profit can be used to pay for things the candidate needs to buy to help get elected.

Answers: Fold under before reproducing this page.

1. $30, 2. $5, 3. $1.50, 4. a. 25¢ b. 50¢ c.25¢

Get Elected!

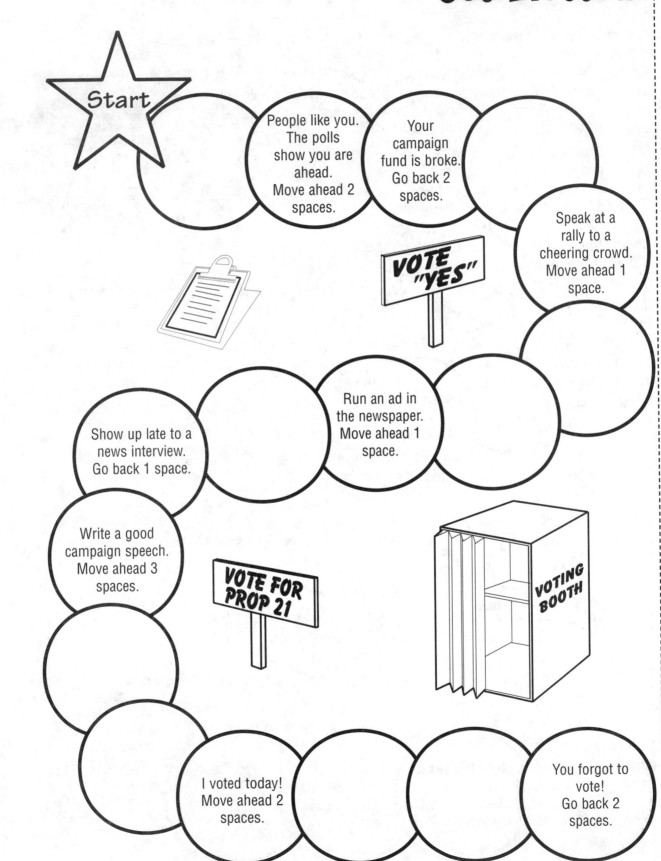

Start

People like you. The polls show you are ahead. Move ahead 2 spaces.

Your campaign fund is broke. Go back 2 spaces.

VOTE "YES"

Speak at a rally to a cheering crowd. Move ahead 1 space.

Run an ad in the newspaper. Move ahead 1 space.

Show up late to a news interview. Go back 1 space.

Write a good campaign speech. Move ahead 3 spaces.

VOTE FOR PROP 21

VOTING BOOTH

I voted today! Move ahead 2 spaces.

You forgot to vote! Go back 2 spaces.

Board Game

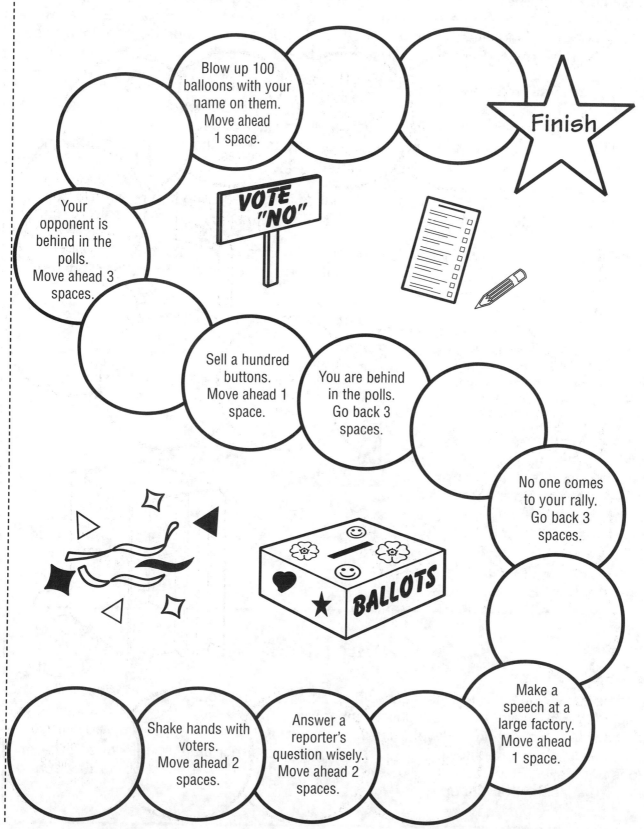

Blow up 100 balloons with your name on them. Move ahead 1 space.

Finish

Your opponent is behind in the polls. Move ahead 3 spaces.

VOTE "NO"

Sell a hundred buttons. Move ahead 1 space.

You are behind in the polls. Go back 3 spaces.

No one comes to your rally. Go back 3 spaces.

BALLOTS

Make a speech at a large factory. Move ahead 1 space.

Shake hands with voters. Move ahead 2 spaces.

Answer a reporter's question wisely. Move ahead 2 spaces.

Board Game Preparation

Board Game Directions: Cut out the two halves of the board game. Glue the pieces together onto a large piece of heavy paper, matching the dashed lines. (**Note:** You may wish to color the board before assembly and laminate it when finished.) Reproduce the game rules at the bottom of this page. Provide a copy for each board game.

Teacher Directions: Write several questions relating to the information students have learned about elections. Place a question on an index card or heavy paper for students to answer. (This is a great way to reinforce the information students have already learned about elections.) Be sure to include an answer key for players to check their responses. Use the cards to play the Get Elected! game on pages 26 and 27.

Sets of questions can be replaced as new information is learned. The board game makes an excellent learning center activity.

Spinner Directions: Prepare a spinner for the game board on pages 26 and 27. Players will spin the spinner to determine the first player and the number of moves on the board game.

To make the spinner, enlarge and reproduce the spinner and arrow patterns on heavy paper and cut them out. Make a hole in the center of the arrow. Place the arrow over the spinner so that the hole is directly over the center dot in the circle. Push the point of a brad (paper fastener) through the dot in the center of the circle. Spread the brad's ends apart. Test the spinner. If the arrow is too tight, adjust the bending points of the brad and/or enlarge the center hole on the arrow.

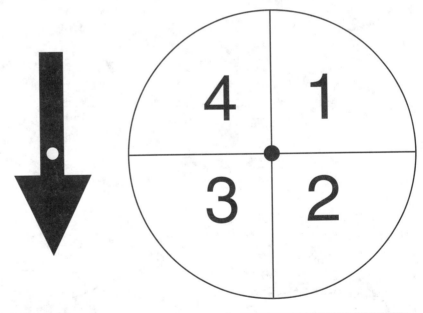

Game Rules

Stack the game (question) cards facedown next to the game board. Each player spins the spinner. The player with the higher number will go first. Player 1 selects the top card and answers the question. (Player 2 checks the answer key.) If correct, Player 1 spins the spinner to determine how many spaces to move his or her marker. If incorrect, Player 1 does not move. Player 2 then follows the same rules to play. The first player to reach the Finish space is the winner.

Making Sense of an Actual Election

If you are teaching this unit during an election year, use the newspaper, television, and news magazines as much as possible to make the elections a concrete event for your young students. Also consider doing the following:

You may wish to put up a calendar that shows how many days until the next election and perhaps even make a chain of paper links, removing one link each day that the election draws nearer.

You can devote a bulletin board to election events. For example, you might label the bulletin board to show pictures of the major candidates. Add another label for each candidate asking, "What do the polls say?" and add articles and pictures of any graphed information. Another section of the board might be labeled, "Hitting the Campaign Trail." In this section, you can add pictures of the candidates speaking at rallies or even add a small map that follows the states that each candidate has visited.

Instead of a teacher-created bulletin board, you might want to have one that is student-generated. Ask students to clip out and bring in captioned photographs of candidates or information taken in polls. Sometimes a photographer will capture an interesting expression on a candidate's face, which can lead to an interesting discussion about body language and the humanity of the candidate.

A pending student council election can be a good learning tool. If students are too young to send a representative to the student council, they can still be part of the process. If possible, arrange to have some of the candidates come to your classroom to explain the job for which they are running for office and to tell your students why they want the job. The older students can leave behind some campaign materials, such as bookmarks or paper buttons.

Encourage your students to think about running for student leadership someday. Who knows? The future student council president might be amongst your students!

Following an Election

When you wish to choose a candidate wisely, you need to have information. Here is a list of some ways to get information. You and your classmates may think of others.

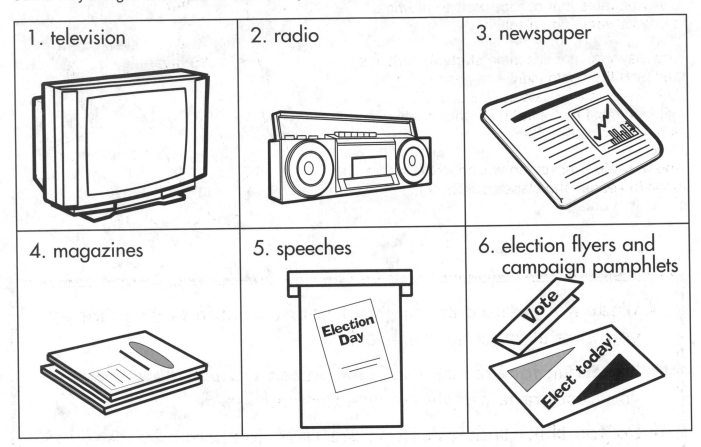

1. television
2. radio
3. newspaper
4. magazines
5. speeches
6. election flyers and campaign pamphlets

Some ways of getting information might be more useful than others. For example, by watching television you can see how a candidate treats other people. Also, a good speaker may make a better leader. By reading the newspaper, however, you can find out what happens every day during an election. You can also get more information from a long newspaper article than from a short television piece.

Speeches and election flyers can give you information, but they are one-sided. That is, you will only be able to learn what the candidate wants you to know. This can be helpful, but you need to know about both candidates to make a good decision. For example, a local candidate may say that he or she wants to see more parks built. This may sound like a good idea to you. But if there are already plans to build parks, then it may be better to vote for someone who has new ideas.

One of the reasons it is so important for children to learn to read is so that when they grow up, they can make good decisions as voters. When someone votes knowing about the candidate, they can feel good about making a choice. When someone votes without information, it does not have much meaning. Remember, voting is a responsibility!

Daily Writing Prompts

There are many writing topics that can be used with this unit. Here is just a sampling of a few prompts that can be used to promote students' writing on elections.

You may wish to collect the students' writings and bind them into individual student books. Ask students to create covers using a patriotic motif to remind them that an election is a national event.

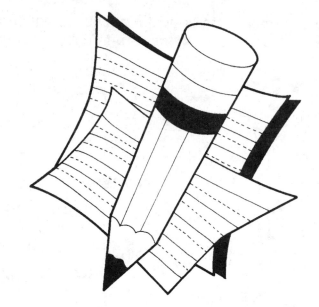

You may also collect the writing into a single book to keep in the classroom library.

- **What would you change about your community or school if you were elected as a leader?**

- **If you ran for President of the United States, how would you encourage people to vote for you?**

- **Do you think that elections are fair? Is there a better way to choose someone as a leader?**

- **How do you and your friends choose a team captain on the playground? Is there a better way?**

- **Do you think anyone who qualifies should be allowed to be President of the United States? Why?**

- **How would you feel if you won an election? If you lost?**

- **Do you think it is fair that elections cost money? How would things be different if candidates received an equal amount of free advertising?**

- **Do you think everyone should vote? Why?**

Elections and Music

When a candidate or a cause wins a long, hard-fought election, then a victory party is in order. Here is a song that is often heard at such a party. Do you know the words and music?

> ### For He's (She's) a Jolly Good Fellow

For he's a jolly good fellow, for he's a jolly good fellow,

for he's a jolly good fellow—which nobody can deny.

Which nobody can deny! Which nobody can deny!

For he's a jolly good fellow, which nobody can deny!

Extensions

As you sing, try substituting names of people in your class for the word "he" or "she" just for fun.

Candidates also sometimes pick songs to remind people who they are during their campaign. Patriotic songs like "God Bless America" and "You're a Grand Old Flag" are often heard at election time. Some candidates choose a different type of song altogether. For example, Bill Clinton chose "Don't Stop Thinking About Tomorrow" by a band called Fleetwood Mac. If you were going to run a campaign, what song might you choose to help people remember you? Why? Write a few sentences about your choice.

Song I would choose: _____

Why I would choose this song: _____

_____

_____

_____

Election Simulation

During this election simulation, divide your class into cooperative groups of 4 or 5 students. Each group will be choosing one of its members to run for president and one of its members for vice president. Remind students of the qualities that make a good leader before students choose their group's candidates. Groups may also choose candidates by picking numbers, drawing straws, etc., to make choosing more impartial for this age level.

Explain the following rules of the simulation.

Campaign Expenses

Each group will be given 10 dollars to spend on campaign expenses. (Use the campaign money template on page 38 to copy enough money for each group, plus extra campaign money earned from the Election Reward Cards on page 42.) The campaign manager will keep track of this money using the accounting worksheet. Each time a transaction—either positive or negative—is made, the accountant should document it on the worksheet. Model this process on the board for your students.

Activities

Each student will have an activity to complete.

❏ **Presidential Candidate and Vice Presidential Candidate:** Create a speech presentation. (This can be similar to a TV commercial, radio commercial, or a Web site.) Student presentations or speeches should take place during class time on a particular day with all group participants being introduced for their contributions to the campaign.

❏ **Artwork Supervisor(s):** Create a poster to advertise for the candidates. If there are more than four members in the cooperative group, then there can be more than one artwork supervisor. The poster should be unveiled at the class presentation and can be displayed in the room thereafter. The artwork supervisor(s) can also color and assemble the campaign bank to hold campaign funds (See page 37 for the pattern. Enlarge and reproduce the pattern onto heavy paper).

❏ **Campaign Manager:** Account for all monetary transactions; register all voters in the group; and oversee speech presentation and poster making.

Election Simulation *(cont.)*

Activities *(cont.)*

❑ **All Cooperative Group Members:** Help to create a polling place by making an individual U.S. flag. Make a ballot box as a group. (A decorated cardboard shoebox or similarly-sized box will do.) Complete the "Election Reflection" activity on page 47.

Supplies

All supplies cost money. Groups will make up their own supply list prices or use the list provided on page 41. The "Supply List" should be posted in the room and used for all election simulation supplies.

Funds

Additional funds can be earned for good behavior. Reward your students by catching them being good and allowing the campaign manager to draw an "Election Reward Card" (page 42) to trade in for campaign dollars. Dollars can be kept in a bank.

Election Celebration

You may wish to end the simulation with a small election party. Students can decorate plain store-bought cookies with white icing and decorate them with sugar confetti dots. Serve "patriotic punch" (lemonade or fruit punch). Sing "For He's (She's) a Jolly Good Fellow" (page 32). Admire the posters, ballot boxes, and banks. Praise the campaign speeches.

Evaluation

Hand out the "Election Reflection" sheet on page 47 for all students to complete when the festivities—and the election—are over and the events have been reviewed.

Cooperative Group Activity

Write the names of the students and their roles in the election.

Our Group: _____   _____

_____   _____

_____   _____

All members will help make a polling place. We will work together to make a ballot box and a bank. Each person will make an American flag.

Roles

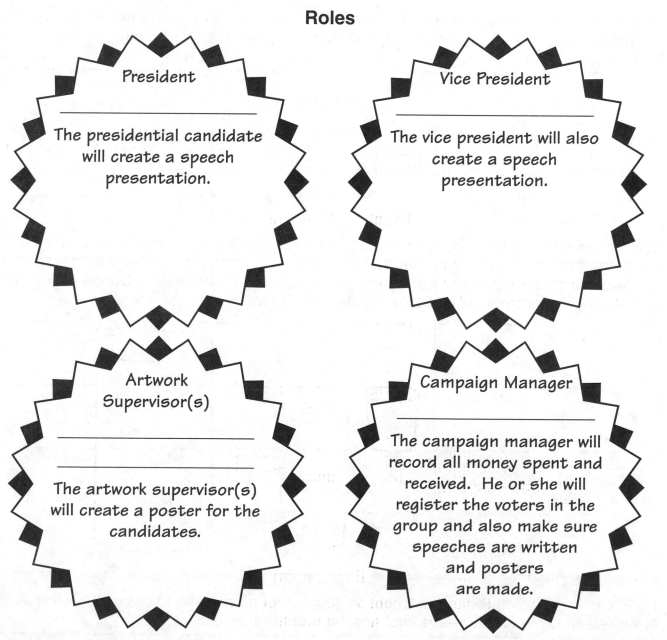

President

_____

The presidential candidate will create a speech presentation.

Vice President

_____

The vice president will also create a speech presentation.

Artwork Supervisor(s)

_____

_____

The artwork supervisor(s) will create a poster for the candidates.

Campaign Manager

_____

The campaign manager will record all money spent and received. He or she will register the voters in the group and also make sure speeches are written and posters are made.

Election Accounting Worksheet

Task for Campaign Manager

The campaign manager must fill out the information on this chart each time money is received or spent. Each group begins with a balance of 10 dollars.

Date	Transaction	Balance
		$10.00

Campaign Bank

Task for Art Supervisor(s)

Color and assemble this bank to hold campaign funds. Cut on the bold lines and then fold on the dotted lines.

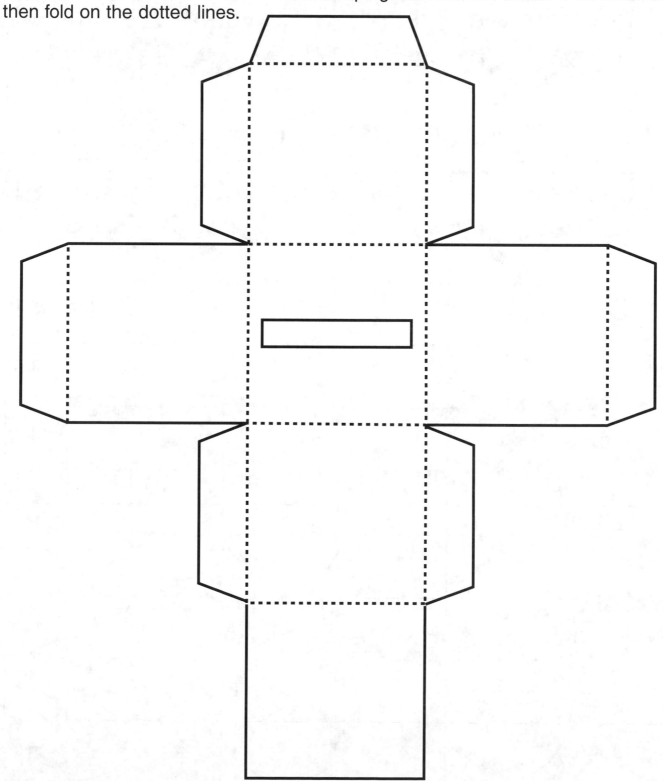

Campaign Money

Copy as many sheets as necessary to supply each group with 10 dollars, plus extra dollars that are earned through the Election Reward Cards (page 42).

$1 In Voters We Trust $1

$1 Campaign Dollar $1

$1 In Voters We Trust $1

$1 Campaign Dollar $1

$1 In Voters We Trust $1

$1 Campaign Dollar $1

$1 In Voters We Trust $1

$1 Campaign Dollar $1

$1 In Voters We Trust $1

$1 Campaign Dollar $1

$1 In Voters We Trust $1

$1 Campaign Dollar $1

In Voters We Trust 25¢

Create a Campaign Speech

Task for Presidential and Vice Presidential Candidates

1. First, decide what type of presentation you will give. Will it be a live speech or for a TV or radio commercial?

2. If it will be a TV or radio commercial, you will need to have the commercial recorded by yourself or an adult helper.

3. If it will be a live speech, rehearse the speech with a friend or an adult helper.

4. Try to come up with a catchy slogan for yourself or your campaign. For example, "John Brown Won't Let You Down!"

5. Write a rough draft of your presentation.

6. When you are finished, show the rough draft to your campaign manager for editing.

Campaign Speech

_____

_____

_____

_____

_____

_____

_____

_____

_____

_____

_____

Create a Campaign Poster

Task for Art Supervisor(s)

Use this sheet to create a rough sketch of your poster idea. Show the poster to the campaign manager for his or her ideas, as well. When you all agree, create a poster for the campaign on poster board. Use markers or other art materials for color. Remember that a good poster is bold and easy to read.

Supply List

Each group may have its own list, or the list can be enlarged and posted in the classroom for reference. Students can "buy" supplies with their campaign money provided on page 38.

Campaign Supplies

	Crayons	25¢
	Markers	50¢
	Poster Board	$1.00
	Poster Paint	$1.00
	Paint Brush	50¢
	Glue	25¢
	Construction Paper	5 sheets for $1.00
	Scissors	50¢
	Stickers	25¢

Election Reward Cards

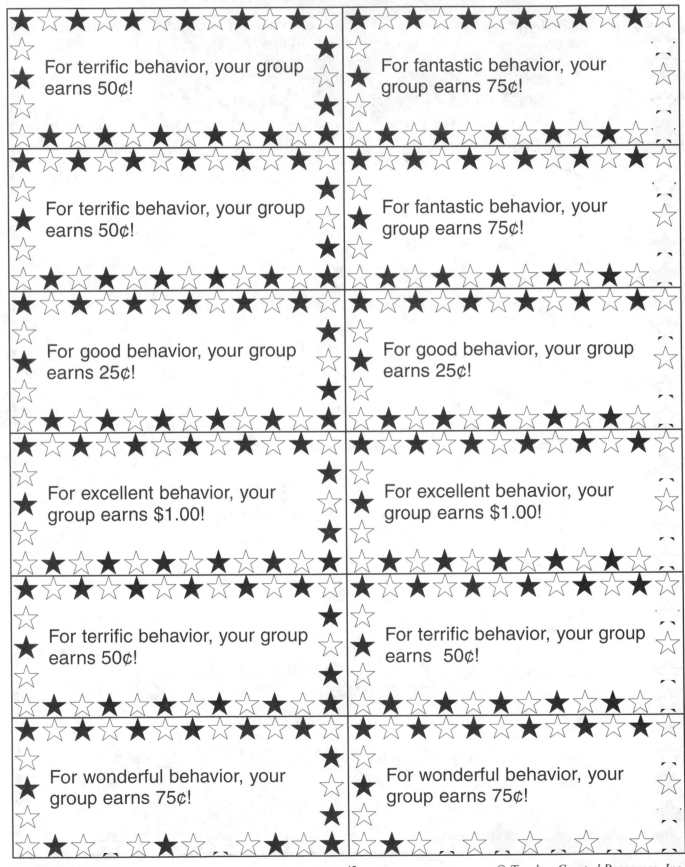

For terrific behavior, your group earns 50¢!

For fantastic behavior, your group earns 75¢!

For terrific behavior, your group earns 50¢!

For fantastic behavior, your group earns 75¢!

For good behavior, your group earns 25¢!

For good behavior, your group earns 25¢!

For excellent behavior, your group earns $1.00!

For excellent behavior, your group earns $1.00!

For terrific behavior, your group earns 50¢!

For terrific behavior, your group earns 50¢!

For wonderful behavior, your group earns 75¢!

For wonderful behavior, your group earns 75¢!

Voter Registration Card

Task for Campaign Manager

All citizens must register in order to vote. Pass out one form to each member of your group. Collect the voter registration cards and turn them in to your teacher. Your teacher will create a list of registered voters to check on election day.

Voter Registration Card

Name _____

_____

Room # _____ Grade _____

Teacher _____

Date _____

_____
(Signature)

Voter Registration Card

Name _____

_____

Room # _____ Grade _____

Teacher _____

Date _____

_____
(Signature)

Voter Registration Card

Name _____

_____

Room # _____ Grade _____

Teacher _____

Date _____

_____
(Signature)

Voter Registration Card

Name _____

_____

Room # _____ Grade _____

Teacher _____

Date _____

_____
(Signature)

Create a Polling Place

Have each student complete one United States flag to decorate the classroom. (Use the template on page 45.) In addition, have each cooperative group work together to create a ballot box by using artwork materials to cover a shoebox, for example, with construction paper or paint. The words "Ballot Box" should appear on the box and there should be a slot in the top for the ballots. (Allow each group to use its own ballot box to vote.) The illustration below shows a polling place for the simulation.

The polling place could include:

- U.S. flag
- state flag
- ballot box (Use one made by a cooperative group.)
- pencils
- ballots
- table
- list of voters to check registration

Create a Flag

Make a United States flag by following the directions below.

Materials

- blue and red markers
- white chalk
- drinking straw for flagpole

		R
		R
		R
		R
		R
		R
		R

Directions

1. Use a blue marker to color the small square.
2. Draw 50 stars using chalk in the small square.
3. Color each space labelled R with red marker.
4. Carefully cut out your flag.
5. Tape your flag to a straw for the flagpole.

Ballot and "I Voted" Tags

Note to Teacher: Make enough copies so that every voter has a ballot and an "I Voted" tag.

Official Election Ballot

Vote for one by placing an "X" by your choice.

_____ ☐

_____ ☐

_____ ☐

_____ ☐

_____ ☐

_____
(date)

Official Election Ballot

Vote for one by placing an "X" by your choice.

_____ ☐

_____ ☐

_____ ☐

_____ ☐

_____ ☐

_____
(date)

Election Reflection

Please answer the following questions after reviewing the election activities you have completed.

1. What was the best part about the elections unit?

_____

_____

_____

2. What did you like the least about the elections unit?

_____

_____

_____

3. How did you feel once the election was over?

_____

_____

_____

4. Tell at least one thing that you learned about elections.

_____

_____

_____

5. Draw a picture showing one activity about elections.

Bibliography

Books

Harvey, Miles. *Presidential Elections (Cornerstones of Freedom Series.)* Children's Press, 1995.

Heath, David. *Elections in the United States.* Capstone, 1998.

Maestro, Betsy C. *The Voice of the People.* Morrow, 1998.

Maestro, Betsy C. *The Voice of the People: American Democracy in Action.* Lothrop, 1996.

Raber, Thomas R. *Election Night (Politics in the United States Series).* Lerner Publications, 1988.

Sher, Linda. *The Vote: Making Your Voice Heard (Good Citizenship Library).* Raintree/Steck-Vaughn, 1996.

Steins, Richard. *Our Elections (I Know America).* Millbrook Paper Trade, 1996.

Web Sites

Kidcafe: Electronic Youth Presidential Poll
http://www.kidlink.org/KIDCAFE/main.html
This site has interactive discussions about presidential candidates in the U.S. and presidential elections.

Kids Voting U.S.A.
http://www.kidsvotingusa.org/
Kids Voting U.S.A. is a nonprofit, nonpartisan organization dedicated to securing democracy for the future by involving children in the election process today.

TIME for Kids
http://www.pathfinder.com/TFK
Online version of the weekly news magazine, written for children.

White House for Kids
http://www.whitehouse.gov/WH/kids/html/kids home.html
Take a child-friendly tour of the White House. You can also send an e-mail to the President.

Answer Key

Page 10

1. ballot
2. political party
3. majority
4. candidate or nominee
5. poll
6. vote
7. candidate
8. cast
9. ballot box

Page 11

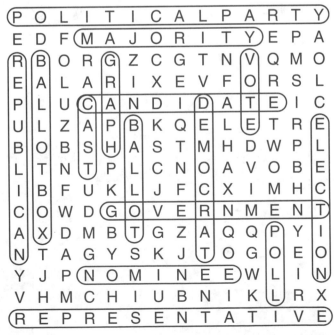